NOT-SO-ORDINARY
SCIENCE

49 PROJECTS THAT OOZE, POP, ZOOM, AND MORE!

by Elsie Olson

CAPSTONE PRESS
a capstone imprint

TABLE OF CONTENTS

MAKE, CREATE, EXPERIMENT!

What happens when chemistry goes kaboom and forces make things zoom? Or when odors reek and experiments create a rocking racket? Science isn't a bore. It's amazingly entertaining! Find out for yourself with these easy hands-on projects that are messy, noisy, smelly, and mobile. So gather your supplies, roll up your sleeves, and get ready for . . .

NOT-SO-ORDINARY SCIENCE FUN!

GENERAL TOOLS & SUPPLIES

baking soda

balloons

bar soap

batteries

cornstarch

crayons

dish soap

drinking straws

duct tape

essential oils

flowers

food coloring

glitter

herbs

hole punch

hot glue gun

liquid starch

measuring cups
& spoons

mini motors

mixing bowl
& spoons

paper cups

pushpins

rubber bands

ruler

school glue

scissors

spices

string

vanilla extract

wire stripper

···· TIPS & TRICKS ····

FOLLOW THESE SIMPLE TIPS TO STAY SAFE AND HAVE FUN!

◆ **Read all the steps** and gather all your supplies before starting a project.

◆ **Ask an adult** to help when using hot or sharp tools.

◆ **Wear eye protection** when working with things that may burst or explode.

◆ **Wash your hands** after handling slime.

◆ **Be smart with essential oils.** Don't swallow oils, put them directly on your skin, or use them around pets. Wear gloves when working with essential oils. And remember that a few drops go a long way!

◆ **Many of the supplies** needed can be found around the house. Others, such as mini motors and magnets, can be purchased at hardware stores or online.

◆ **Check the meter** at the start of each project to see how messy, noisy, smelly, or mobile it will be.

◆ **Making a messy project?** Wear old clothing and make sure to protect your work area with newspaper, a drop cloth, or a tarp. Better yet, go outside!

◆ **Making a noisy project?** Make sure those around you don't mind a little noise. Try experimenting during the day.

◆ **Making a smelly project?** Be considerate of others and ask if they're okay with a few extra smells in the air.

◆ **Making a project that moves?** Check that your work area is large enough so projects don't cause injury or damage.

FOAMING SWAMP MONSTER

When molecules break up, things can get messy! Use chemistry to make a monster **spew slime and froth foam.**

WHAT YOU NEED

- clean, empty can
- art supplies, such as felt, googly eyes & glue
- ½ cup (118 milliliters) hydrogen peroxide
- ¼ cup (59 mL) dish soap
- food coloring
- paper cup or other container for mixing
- mixing spoon
- active yeast
- ½ cup (118 mL) warm water
- measuring cups & spoons

STEP 1

Decorate a clean, empty can to look like a monster.

STEP 2

In the can, mix together the hydrogen peroxide, dish soap, and a few drops of food coloring.

STEP 3

In a separate container, mix together one packet of active yeast and the warm water. Let the mixture sit for at least five minutes.

STEP 4

Pour the yeast mixture into the can, and watch your monster foam!

WHAT YOU GET

A chemical reaction! Hydrogen peroxide is unstable. It wants to break into two parts, water and oxygen. This reaction normally takes time. But yeast causes the reaction to happen quickly. Dish soap captures the oxygen as it breaks from the hydrogen peroxide. This creates foam. **That's science!**

SLIME BUBBLES

This crystal-clear slime is just the beginning. What happens when you let your slime sit for a few days? Wait and see!

WHAT YOU NEED

- ½ cup (118 mL) clear school glue
- ¼ teaspoon (1.2 mL) baking soda
- saline contact solution containing boric acid
- mixing bowl & spoon
- measuring cups & spoons

STEP 1

Mix the clear school glue with the baking soda. Stir well.

STEP 2

Stir in the saline solution a few drops at a time until a ball forms. Coat your hands in saline solution and knead the ball until it becomes a smooth, nonsticky slime.

STEP 3

Set the slime aside. Let it sit covered for five to seven days.

WHAT YOU GET

Bubbles, baby! As the slime sits, air bubbles rise to the top. The slime is too thick for the air bubbles to escape right away. So, they form a layer on top. **That's science!**

HOT & COLD WATER STACK

Can you stack water without it mixing? Try to stay dry as you perfect this **topsy-turvy experiment!**

MESS-O-METER
5

WHAT YOU NEED

- plastic container, such as a milk jug or soda bottle
- scissors or craft knife
- 2 glasses of the same size
- food coloring (2 colors)
- water
- mixing spoon

EXPERIMENT! TRY STACKING COLD WATER ON TOP OF HOT WATER. WHAT HAPPENS?

STEP 1

Cut a circle out of the plastic container. The circle should be big enough to completely cover the top of the glass.

STEP 2

Fill one glass with hot water. Stir in food coloring. Fill the other glass with cold water. Stir in a different color of food coloring.

STEP 3

Place the plastic circle on top of the hot-water glass. Carefully turn the glass over while holding the plastic firmly. Set the glass on top of the cold-water glass.

STEP 4

Carefully slide the plastic circle out from between the two glasses. Make sure to hold the top glass in place!

WHAT YOU GET

Density at work! Hot water is less dense than cold water. This allows the hot water to sit on top of the cold water without mixing in. **That's science!**

OOEY GOOEY ROCKS

MESS-O-METER
5

Gather your glue and make some rock-filled slime that's ready to **roll onto the construction site.**

WHAT YOU NEED

- ⅔ cup (158 mL) clear school glue
- ½ cup (118 mL) liquid starch, plus extra
- pebbles
- mixing bowl & spoon
- measuring cups & spoons

STEP 1

Stir together the clear school glue and liquid starch.

STEP 2

Add more liquid starch 1 tablespoon (15 mL) at a time until a ball forms. Knead the ball, adding starch as necessary until you have made a smooth, nonsticky slime.

STEP 3

Mix several dozen pebbles into the slime until the mixture can stand on its own.

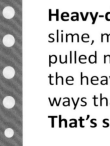

WHAT YOU GET

Heavy-duty slime! The pebbles add mass to the slime, making it heavier. Heavier objects are pulled more strongly by gravity. So, the heavy slime moves in different ways than a lighter slime would. **That's science!**

GLITTER BOUNCY BALLS

Polymers are long chains of molecules. Rubber, plastic, and nylon are all polymers you probably use every day! Use polymers to make your own **sparkly bouncy balls!**

WHAT YOU NEED

- ¼ cup (59 mL) warm water
- 2 teaspoons (10 mL) borax
- paper cup
- ¼ cup (59 mL) school glue
- 4 teaspoons (20 mL) cornstarch
- food coloring
- glitter
- plate
- mixing bowl & spoon
- measuring cups & spoons

Borax
(Sodium Tetraborate)
≥ 99.9 %

EXPERIMENT! TRY ADDING MORE OR LESS OF THE BORAX SOLUTION. WHAT HAPPENS?

STEP 1

Mix together the warm water and borax in a paper cup.

STEP 2

Mix together the school glue and cornstarch in a small bowl. Add food coloring and glitter to the mixture.

STEP 3

Add 2 teaspoons (10 mL) of the borax mixture to the glue mixture. Stir until it begins to solidify. Then, knead the mixture with your hands until a stiff dough forms.

STEP 4

Break off small chunks of dough and roll them into balls. The more you handle the dough, the stiffer it will get. Roll each ball in glitter. Then, give the balls a bounce! Store the balls in an airtight container when done using.

WHAT YOU GET

The power of polymers! The polymers in glue normally slide past each other. But the borax mixture makes the glue's polymers stick together. This causes the glue to become more solid and elastic. Cornstarch thickens the glue and helps the bouncy balls hold their shape. **That's science!**

CHALK BOMB

Harness the power of chemistry to make a colorful explosion. (This one is extra messy, so you may want to take it outside!)

WHAT YOU NEED

- colored sidewalk chalk
- plastic zipper-close bags
- hammer
- 1 tablespoon (15 mL) baking soda
- ¼ cup (59 mL) vinegar
- measuring cups & spoons

STEP 1

Place several pieces of chalk in a plastic bag. You can use just one color or combine colors!

STEP 2

Place the chalk bag on a hard surface, such as pavement. Use a hammer to smash the chalk into a fine powder.

STEP 3

If the bag is damaged from hammering, transfer the powder to a new bag. Add the baking soda to the bag.

STEP 4

Pour the vinegar into the bag and seal it tightly. Then, stand back and wait!

WHAT YOU GET

Kaboom! Sidewalk chalk and baking soda are bases. Vinegar is an acid. When the three substances mix, the acid causes the bases to release carbon dioxide. This gas expands until the bag explodes. **That's science!**

FIERCE FOUNTAIN

MESS-O-METER

With just a balloon, a bottle, and a drinking straw, you can fashion a fierce fountain that spews colorful liquid. **Prepare to get wet!**

WHAT YOU NEED

- pushpin
- clear plastic water or soda bottle
- ballpoint pen
- drinking straw
- mounting putty
- water
- blue food coloring
- art supplies, such as a paper cup, duct tape, craft foam & more
- balloon

EXPERIMENT! WHAT HAPPENS IF YOU MAKE THE WATER LEVEL HIGHER THAN THE STRAW?

20

STEP 1

Use a pushpin to poke a hole near the middle of a plastic water or soda bottle. Use a ballpoint pen to make the hole large enough for a drinking straw to fit through.

STEP 2

Insert the straw into the hole. Seal the seam between the bottle and straw with mounting putty.

STEP 3

Pour water into the bottle until it is just below the outer end of the straw. Add blue food coloring to color the water. Use a paper cup to decorate the end of the straw to look like a dragon or another animal.

STEP 4

Blow up a balloon. Keeping the end pinched closed, wrap the balloon opening around the mouth of the bottle. Stand back!

WHAT YOU GET

Air pressure at work! As the balloon deflates, its air rushes into the bottle. The force of the air pushes down on the water and forces it up through the straw. **That's science!**

21

EXPLODING WATERMELON

MESS-O-METER

Grab your goggles and get ready for some wet and wild watermelon fun. Don't forget to enjoy a bite of melon **after the explosion!**

WHAT YOU NEED

- ◆ drop cloth or tarp (optional)
- ◆ eye protection
- ◆ watermelon
- ◆ rubber bands (about 100)

STEP 1

Spread out a tarp or drop cloth, if using, and put on eye protection.

STEP 2

Stretch a rubber band around the center of the watermelon.

STEP 3

Keep adding rubber bands. Pay attention as the watermelon changes shape and starts to bulge. Be patient! This may take time.

STEP 4

When you see the first large crack start to form in the melon, stand back. Your melon is about to blow!

WHAT YOU GET

Fruit under pressure! Each rubber band exerts a small amount of force on the melon. As you add more rubber bands, the force becomes greater. Eventually, it becomes so great that the melon explodes. **That's science!**

PAINT SPLATTER ART

You may want to dig out some old clothes for this art project. When paint and potential energy meet, **things will get messy!**

MESS-O-METER

WHAT YOU NEED

- pushpins
- white tagboard
- tarp or drop cloth (optional)
- balloons
- funnel
- ¼ cup (59 mL) washable, nontoxic paint
- measuring cups & spoons

▲ ▲ ▲

EXPERIMENT! TRY DROPPING THE BALLOON FROM DIFFERENT HEIGHTS. DOES IT CHANGE YOUR SPLATTER ART?

▼ ▼ ▼

STEP 1

Insert pushpins through a white sheet of tagboard. Turn the tagboard over and place it pointy side up on a tarp, drop cloth, or grassy area that can get messy.

STEP 2

Stretch a balloon by inflating it and letting the air out. Insert a funnel into the end of the balloon. Pour the paint through the funnel and into the balloon.

STEP 3

Inflate the paint-filled balloon and tie the end.

Repeat **steps 2 and 3** to fill additional balloons.

STEP 4

Drop the balloons onto the pins and watch the paint splatter!

WHAT YOU GET

Energy in action! An inflated balloon stores potential energy. When the balloon pops, the potential energy converts into motion, sending the paint inside the balloon flying. **That's science!**

ICKY TAR PIT

MESS-O-METER
4

Long ago, prehistoric animals became trapped in thick pools of tar. Create a special slime to mimic a dangerous tar pit!

WHAT YOU NEED

- 1 cup (0.24 liters) cornstarch
- ½ cup (118 mL) warm water
- black paint
- mixing bowl & spoon
- measuring cups & spoons
- plate
- plastic toys, sand & fake plants (optional)

▲ ▲ ▲
EXPERIMENT! TRY ADDING MORE LIQUID OR LESS CORNSTARCH. WHAT HAPPENS?
▼ ▼ ▼

STEP 1

Mix together the cornstarch and warm water.

STEP 2

Stir in a few tablespoons of black paint until the mixture is tar colored.

ACRYLIC PAINT

BLACK
25mL

STEP 3

Continue stirring until the mixture thickens. Then, mix with your hands until you can squeeze the mixture into a ball.

STEP 4

Spread your "tar" out on a plate. If you like, add plastic toys, sand, and fake plants to your tar pit!

WHAT YOU GET

A non-Newtonian fluid! The substance you made isn't a liquid or a solid. When placed on top, toys sink as if into liquid. But if you poke or flick the substance, it feels solid. **That's science!**

COLOR-SHIFTING SLIME

Baby bottles, mood rings, and receipts all use thermochromic pigments to change color when exposed to heat. Mix up a batch of cool slime that gets even cooler **the warmer it gets.**

WHAT YOU NEED

- ¼ cup (59 mL) white school glue
- 1 tablespoon (15 mL) water
- food coloring (optional)
- 1 tablespoon (15 mL) thermochromic pigment
- ½ cup (118 mL) liquid starch
- mixing bowl & spoon
- measuring cups & spoons
- hot and cold items, such as a blow-dryer & ice pack

STEP 1
Stir together white school glue and water. Add food coloring if you'd like.

STEP 2
Add the thermochromic pigment to the mixture. Stir well.

STEP 3
Add ¼ cup (59 mL) of liquid starch. Stir to combine.

STEP 4
Add another ¼ cup (59 mL) of starch little by little. Knead the mixture until it is smooth, stretchy, and no longer sticks to your fingers.

STEP 5
Change the temperature and color of your slime by using a blow-dryer, ice pack, and more!

WHAT YOU GET

Harnessed heat! Thermochromic pigment is made from special dyes or tiny crystals. When exposed to heat, the molecules in these substances change position. This causes the pigment to change color. **That's science!**

SCULPTABLE SAND

Mix up a batch of sand that you can mold, shape, and sculpt! What will you build?

WHAT YOU NEED

- ⅔ cup (158 mL) clear school glue
- ½ cup (118 mL) liquid starch, plus extra
- 1 cup (0.24 L) fine sand, plus extra
- mixing bowls & spoon
- measuring cups & spoons

STEP 1
Stir together the clear school glue and liquid starch.

STEP 2
Continue adding liquid starch 1 tablespoon (15 mL) at a time until a ball forms. Knead the ball, adding more starch as needed until it becomes a smooth and nonsticky slime.

STEP 3
In a separate bowl, use your hands to mix together the sand and half the slime. The mixture should be soft enough to mold but solid enough to hold a shape. Add more sand or slime until the mixture is the right consistency.

WHAT YOU GET

Flow like a liquid, squeeze like a solid! Mixing glue and starch makes a non-Newtonian slime. When the slime coats the sand, the sand acts like the slime. So, you can shape the sand into sculptures, blocks, and more. **That's science!**

SQUEEZE & SPLAT EGGS

MESS-O-METER
8

With a little vinegar and a little time, you can turn a raw egg into a **smelly, bouncy, rubbery mess!**

WHAT YOU NEED

- clear plastic cups
- raw eggs
- vinegar
- food coloring
- white tagboard

▲ ▲ ▲

EXPERIMENT! LET YOUR EGGS SIT FOR DIFFERENT AMOUNTS OF TIME. HOW DOES THE EXPERIMENT CHANGE AS THE EGG SITS LONGER?

▼ ▼ ▼

STEP 1

Place an egg into each cup. Add enough vinegar to each cup to cover the egg. Add a few drops of food coloring to the vinegar.

STEP 2

Let the eggs sit in the vinegar for three to seven days.

3–7 DAYS

STEP 3

Remove the eggs from the cups. What do they feel like? Drop the eggs from different heights onto white tagboard. Do the eggs bounce or burst? What color are the yolks?

WHAT YOU GET

Colorful, rubbery eggs! Vinegar is acidic. It dissolves the hard part of the eggshell, leaving behind a soft, rubbery membrane. The colored vinegar flows through this membrane and colors the egg. But proteins in the egg yolk keep the yolk from absorbing any color. So, it stays yellow. **That's science!**

DANCING GLITTER

NOISE-O-METER

5

Make some glitter hop and groove when you sing into a cardboard tube!

- paper towel tube
- scissors
- pencil
- plastic or cardboard container
- duct tape
- balloon
- craft knife
- art supplies, such as glue, googly eyes & construction paper
- glitter

▲ ▲ ▲

EXPERIMENT! TRY SINGING AT DIFFERENT PITCHES AND VOLUMES. WHAT HAPPENS?

▼ ▼ ▼

STEP 1

Cut a paper towel tube in half horizontally on a diagonal. Tape the halves back together at an angle.

STEP 2

Trace one end of the tube onto the plastic or cardboard container. Cut out the hole using a craft knife.

STEP 3

Poke one end of the angled tube through the hole and tape it in place to secure.

STEP 4

Cut the tip off the balloon and stretch it over the container's opening. Decorate the container!

STEP 5

Pour glitter on top of the balloon. Sing into the tube and watch the glitter dance and bounce!

WHAT YOU GET

Membrane motion. The balloon stretched across the container is a membrane. As you sing into the tube, the vibrations from your voice cause air inside the container to vibrate the membrane. This causes the glitter to bounce around. **That's science!**

UNDERWATER BELL

NOISE-O-METER 3

A whale's song can be heard from thousands of miles away. How does sound travel so well underwater? Make a waterproof bell to find out!

WHAT YOU NEED

- clean tin can
- art supplies
- hammer & nail
- wire
- scissors
- ruler
- small bells
- tub or sink full of water

EXPERIMENT! TRY THIS AT A BEACH OR IN A POOL. DUNK YOUR HEAD AND RING THE BELL. WHAT DO YOU HEAR?

STEP 1

Decorate a tin can. Use a hammer and nail to poke a hole through the can's bottom.

STEP 2

Cut a length of wire 6 inches (15 centimeters) long and twist one end around the hangers of two small bells.

STEP 3

Poke the untwisted end of the wire into the tin can and up through the hole. Twist to secure. Ring the bell and listen to what it sounds like.

STEP 4

Now ring the bell underwater. How is the sound different?

WHAT YOU GET

A different kind of wave. Sound travels in waves. These waves are created by vibrations. Waves travel more quickly in dense substances, and faster waves make a noise seem louder. Water is denser than air. So, the bell sounds louder and clearer underwater. **That's science!**

FANCY FLUTE

NOISE-O-METER
3

A few straws, some cardboard, and a bit of tape are all you need to make beautiful music!

WHAT YOU NEED

- 4 drinking straws
- scissors

- cardboard
- ruler
- duct tape

STEP 1

Cut the straws so they are all slightly different lengths.

STEP 2

Cut two strips of cardboard about 1 inch (2.5 cm) wide and 6 inches (15 cm) long. Cut two pieces of duct tape slightly shorter than the cardboard.

STEP 3

Roll each piece of tape lengthwise with the sticky side out. Place each tape roll on a cardboard strip. Place the straws shortest to longest on one piece of tape, lining up the tops of the straws.

STEP 4

Place the second cardboard strip sticky side down on top of the straws so it lines up with the bottom strip.

STEP 5

Blow across the straw openings to make sound. How does the sound change as you blow across the different straw lengths?

WHAT YOU GET

Perfect pitch. When you blow air across a straw opening, the air vibrates inside the straw, making sound. The wavelength of the vibrations changes depending on the straw's length. This creates different pitches. **That's science!**

NOT-SO-MOBILE PHONE

Which type of string carries sound the best? Find out with this cup-and-string sound experiment!

NOISE-O-METER
3

WHAT YOU NEED

- 6 to 8 paper or plastic cups
- pushpin
- sharpened pencil
- scissors
- ruler
- different types of wire or string, such as yarn, thread & twine
- partner

▲ ▲ ▲
EXPERIMENT! WHAT HAPPENS WHEN YOU USE DIFFERENT LENGTHS OF STRING?
▼ ▼ ▼

STEP 1

Use a pushpin to poke a hole in the bottoms of two cups. Use a sharpened pencil to widen the hole as needed.

STEP 2

Cut a length of string 8 to 10 feet (2 to 3 meters) long.

STEP 3

Poke each end of the string up through the bottom of a cup and knot inside the cup to secure.

Repeat **steps 1 through 3** using other types of string.

STEP 4

Give a partner one cup. Stand far away from each other so the string between the cups is stretched tight. Have your partner speak into their cup while you hold your cup to your ear.

STEP 5

Speak and listen with each cup and string set. How does the sound change?

WHAT YOU GET

Vibrations on the move. When you speak into the cup, your voice vibrates the air inside. These vibrations pass through the bottom of the cup, down the string, and into the other cup. Thin, tight strings carry sound better than thick, loose strings. **That's science!**

WAILING BALLOON

Is there a ghost in the lab? Roll a hex nut and other objects around inside a balloon for some spooky sound effects!

WHAT YOU NEED

- balloons
- hex nuts
- other small objects, such as pebbles, dice & marbles

▲ ▲ ▲

EXPERIMENT! TRY BLOWING UP THE BALLOONS TO DIFFERENT SIZES. HOW DOES THE SOUND CHANGE?

▼ ▼ ▼

STEP 1

Insert a hex nut through a balloon's neck. Blow up the balloon and tie the end.

STEP 2

Hold the tied end of the balloon in your palm. Rotate the balloon until the hex nut starts rolling around.

STEP 3

Keep rotating the balloon, building up speed until you start hearing a spooky noise. Then stop rotating the balloon. What happens?

STEP 4

Try this experiment again with other small objects. How does the sound change?

WHAT YOU GET

Forces and motion. As the six sides of the hex nut roll inside the balloon, they vibrate against the balloon wall, making a wailing sound. Centripetal force keeps the hex nut spinning even after you've stopped rotating the balloon. **That's science!**

STELLAR XYLOPHONE

Make some **beautiful music** while learning how water affects pitch!

NOISE-O-METER
5

WHAT YOU NEED

- 4 to 6 identical glass jars
- water
- food coloring
- art supplies, such as chenille stems, googly eyes & glue
- metal spoon

EXPERIMENT! BUILD A SIMILAR XYLOPHONE USING DIFFERENT LIQUIDS. TRY JUICE OR MILK!

STEP 1

Fill each jar with a different amount of water.

STEP 2

Add a different food coloring to each jar. If you'd like, decorate your jars to look like aliens or other creatures.

STEP 3

Lightly tap a metal spoon against the side of each jar. What do you notice?

WHAT YOU GET

Switching pitches. Tapping the spoon against the jars creates vibrations. Water slows down the movement of the vibrations. Slower vibrations make lower pitches. So, the glass with the most water will have the lowest pitch. **That's science!**

FLYING BUZZER

Make a nifty noisemaker that sounds just like a **buzzing swarm of insects!**

NOISE-O-METER 6

WHAT YOU NEED

- 2 index cards
- clear tape
- craft stick
- craft foam
- ruler
- scissors
- string
- wide rubber band

▲ ▲ ▲

EXPERIMENT! CUT SMALL SLITS ALONG THE EDGES OF THE INDEX CARDS. WHAT HAPPENS?

▽ ▽ ▽

STEP 1

Tape an index card to either side of a craft stick.

STEP 2

Cut two strips of craft foam, each 4 inches (10 cm) long and the width of the craft stick.

STEP 3

Fold one craft foam strip in half widthwise. Fold the strip again around the end of the craft stick and tape it in place. Repeat on the other side of the craft stick.

STEP 4

Cut a string 3 feet (0.9 m) long and tie it to one end of the craft stick, over the craft foam. Stretch a rubber band across the length of the craft stick and craft foam.

STEP 5

Use the string to spin the buzzer around in circles. What happens?

WHAT YOU GET

Vibration amplification. When you swing the noisemaker around, the air vibrates the rubber band, making a buzzing noise. The index cards amplify the sound, or make it louder. **That's science!**

SCREECHING OWL

NOISE-O-METER
6

Use the science of sound to turn a regular foam cup into a screeching snowy owl pal!

WHAT YOU NEED

- string
- scissors
- ruler
- sponge
- pushpin
- foam cup
- sharpened pencil
- paper clip
- art supplies, such as markers, glue & feathers
- water

▲ ▲ ▲
EXPERIMENT! TRY USING DIFFERENT STRINGS. HOW DO THE SOUNDS CHANGE?
▼ ▼ ▼

STEP 1

Cut a piece of string 12 inches (30.5 cm) long. Cut the sponge to make a piece about 1 to 2 inches (2.5 to 5 cm) wide.

STEP 2

Tie one end of the string around the sponge piece. Tie a small loop in the other end of the string.

STEP 3

Poke a hole through the bottom of the cup with a pushpin.

STEP 4

Use a sharpened pencil to widen the hole until it is large enough to insert the looped end of the string through. Attach a paper clip to the loop. Decorate the cup to look like an owl.

STEP 5

Wet the sponge and squeeze it around the string inside the cup. Pull down firmly and quickly. What happens?

WHAT YOU GET

Fun with friction. When you pull the wet sponge down the string, the friction from the sponge vibrates the string. The vibrations also travel through the air around the string. The cup's shape helps amplify the vibrations, making them louder. **That's science!**

BOX & BAND GUITAR

Let's make some music!
Use cardboard and rubber bands to make your own playable guitar.

WHAT YOU NEED

- shallow cardboard box with lid
- duct tape
- bowl
- pencil
- craft knife
- long, sturdy cardboard tube
- brass brads
- 4 to 6 rubber bands of various thicknesses
- pushpins
- art supplies

STEP 1

Tape the box lid closed if necessary. Place a bowl in the center of the box and trace around it. Cut out the circle.

STEP 2

Press one end of the cardboard tube against a short end of the box. Trace around the tube and cut out the circle.

STEP 3

Slide the cardboard tube a few inches into the hole. Use brads or duct tape to secure it.

STEP 4

Cut the rubber bands. Poke small holes near the top of the cardboard tube. Thread one end of each rubber band through the holes and knot to secure. Stretch the rubber bands beneath the large hole and use pushpins to secure them. This makes guitar strings.

STEP 5

Tape the ends of the rubber bands to secure. Decorate your guitar. Then pluck the strings!

WHAT YOU GET

Shimmying strings. When you pluck a rubber band, it vibrates. Energy from the vibrations travels across the box and into the hollow body, which amplifies the sound. Thicker rubber bands vibrate more slowly, making lower pitches.
That's science!

SOUNDPROOF HEADPHONES

Sometimes we need *peace and quiet!* Make your own soundproof headphones with everyday materials.

WHAT YOU NEED

- paper towel tube
- scissors
- ruler
- yarn
- hot glue gun
- 2 fillable plastic eggs
- pencil
- cardboard
- headband
- radio, speaker, or other music player
- cotton balls

▲ ▲ ▲

EXPERIMENT! TRY OTHER SOUNDPROOFING MATERIALS, SUCH AS BUBBLE WRAP, FOAM, FABRIC, AND MORE!

▼ ▼ ▼

STEP 1
Cut two rings about 1 inch (2.5 cm) wide out of a paper towel tube. Wrap each ring in yarn, gluing in place as needed.

STEP 2
Trace an egg top two times on cardboard to make two circles. Cut them out.

STEP 3
Wrap the headband and cardboard circles in yarn, gluing in place as needed.

STEP 4
Glue the rings to the rims of two egg tops. Glue each egg top to one end of the headband, making headphones.

STEP 5
Turn on music. Put on your headphones. What do you hear? Next, try filling the headphones with cotton balls. Push the yarn-covered circles into the rings to cover the cotton balls. What do you hear now?

WHAT YOU GET

Sound stoppers. Sound travels easily through some materials, like water and air. Other materials, like cotton and yarn, absorb sound vibrations. They can be used to block sound. **That's science!**

DIFFERENT DRUMS

Get ready to march to the beat of your own drum! This fun sound experiment is the perfect way to **play with pitch!**

WHAT YOU NEED

- balloons
- scissors
- 3 to 4 containers of different sizes
- rubber bands
- art supplies
- 2 pencils with erasers

STEP 1

Cut the neck off a balloon. Stretch the balloon over the opening of a container to make a drum.

STEP 2

Wrap a rubber band around the container to secure the balloon.

Repeat steps 1 and 2 for each container.

STEP 3

Decorate your drum set!

STEP 4

Use the eraser end of pencils to beat the drums. How does the sound change between drums?

WHAT YOU GET

The power of pitch. Because your containers are different sizes, some balloons are stretched tighter than others. The tightness of a drum's skin affects its pitch. The tighter the skin, the higher the pitch. Loose skin makes a lower pitch. **That's science!**

DOPPLER CATCH

Find a pal and play a noisy game of catch to learn about **physics at work!**

NOISE-O-METER

10

WHAT YOU NEED

- plastic ball
- craft knife
- duct tape
- hook-and-loop tape
- ruler
- small battery-powered buzzer or other noisemaker
- partner

STEP 1

Cut the ball in half. Match the two halves back together. Place a small strip of duct tape between them to make a hinge.

STEP 2

Use duct tape to cover the rough edges of each half of the ball.

STEP 3

Attach three small strips of hook-and-loop tape next to the ball's opening, opposite the hinge.

STEP 4

Fold three 3-inch (8 cm) pieces of duct tape in half lengthwise, sticky sides in. Stick a piece of hook-and-loop tape to one end of each strip. Tape the other ends of the strips to the side of the ball without hook-and-loop tape. Attach the hook-and-loop tape pieces together to make flaps.

STEP 5

Cover the rest of the ball in duct tape. Turn on the buzzer and put it in the ball. Close the flaps. Toss the ball back and forth to a partner. How does the sound change?

WHAT YOU GET

The Doppler effect. As a source of sound gets closer to a listener, the frequency of the sound waves increases. This means the sound's pitch gets higher. As the source moves away, the pitch gets lower. This is known as the Doppler effect. **That's science!**

PETITE PIANO

Explore sound waves and pitch by making a pocket-sized piano. This itty-bitty instrument packs a punch!

WHAT YOU NEED

- small, sturdy cardboard box with a lid
- tape
- scissors
- 2 craft sticks
- hot glue gun
- 5 bobby pins

STEP 1

Tape the box lid closed if necessary. Cut a hole in the top of the box.

STEP 2

Trim two craft sticks to the box's width. Glue one craft stick to the box above the hole.

STEP 3

Pry the bobby pins apart at different angles. Arrange them on the craft stick in order of angle size.

STEP 4

Tape the straight ends of the bobby pins to the craft stick so the pins hang over the hole. Glue the other craft stick on top of the bobby pins so it lines up with the first craft stick.

STEP 5

Flick the top of each bobby pin downward quickly. What do you hear?

WHAT YOU GET

All about angles. When you flick the bobby pin, it vibrates the air around it. The box amplifies the sound. The bobby pins at smaller angles create faster vibrations when flicked. This produces higher pitches. **That's science!**

SCENTED BUBBLES

Make colorful bubbles that **smell sweet** as they pop!

EXPERIMENT! MAKE DIFFERENT WAND SHAPES. DO SOME WORK BETTER THAN OTHERS?

WHAT YOU NEED

- pitcher
- 1 cup (0.24 L) unscented dish soap
- 1½ tablespoons (22 mL) glycerin
- 6 cups (1.4 L) water
- mixing spoon
- 3 jars with lids
- food coloring
- essential oils
- chenille stems

STEP 1

In the pitcher, mix together dish soap, glycerin, and water.

STEP 2

Divide the mixture between the three jars. Add different food coloring and essential oils to each jar.

STEP 3

Bend a chenille stem in half. Twist the ends together, making a loop a few inches from the top. This is your bubble wand.

STEP 4

Pour a bit of scented liquid into each jar lid. Dip the wand into the liquid and blow a bubble. Try each scent. Which bubbles smell the strongest?

WHAT YOU GET

Molecule magic! From freshly baked bread to stinky garbage, every object you smell gives off odor molecules. These molecules are usually lightweight enough to travel through the air. When you blow a bubble, it releases essential oil molecules, dispersing the scent! **That's science!**

TRASH MONSTER STINK BOMB

Turn regular kitchen items into a DIY trash monster with a **stench so strong** it's sure to clear a room!

WHAT YOU NEED

- container with lid
- raw egg

- 1 tablespoon (15 mL) milk
- 1 tablespoon (15 mL) vinegar
- art supplies, such as a hot glue gun, aluminum foil, chenille stems & more

STEP 1

Break the egg and drop it into the container.

STEP 2

Add the milk and vinegar. Put the lid on the container and give it a shake to mix up the ingredients.

STEP 3

5-7 DAYS

If you'd like, decorate the container to look like a trash monster or other icky creature. Then put the container in a safe place for five to seven days. The longer it sits, the stinkier it gets!

STEP 4

Remove the lid from your container and leave it where someone can smell it but not see it. Pee-ew!

WHAT YOU GET

Stinky for safety. Bacteria grow on food as it spoils. Both the bacteria and the rotting food release chemicals that smell bad. Bad smells like rotten eggs, spoiled milk, or moldy fruit are a signal to your brain. They tell you something is unsafe and could make you sick. **That's science!**

SMELLY SOAP EXPLOSION

What happens when you put soap in the microwave? Try this **soap-scented experiment** to find out!

SMELL-O-METER 5

WHAT YOU NEED

- Ivory brand bar soap
- another brand of bar soap
- tub or sink filled with water
- plate
- sharp knife & cutting board
- microwave

STEP 1

Place both soaps in the water.
Note whether they float or sink.

STEP 2

Cut a 1-inch (2.5 cm) piece
off each type of soap and
put on a plate.

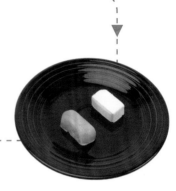

STEP 3

Microwave the soaps for 1 minute.
What happens? How did the floating
soap react differently than the
non-floating soap?

WHAT YOU GET

Expanding soap. Air is whipped into Ivory soap as it is
manufactured. This makes it less dense than water, so it
floats. The tiny air pockets contain water molecules. When
heated, the water expands in the air pockets. This makes the
soap puff. **That's science!**

MEMORY MATCH GAME

How much does your nose know? Find out how good your **scent memory** is with this fun game!

WHAT YOU NEED

- 6 small items with strong scents, such as powdered spices, herbs, or dryer sheets
- 12 identical note cards
- art supplies, such as markers
- glue stick

STEP 1

Collect six different scented items. They should be small and flat enough to fit on the backs of note cards. Items could include powdered spices, herbs, or dryer sheets.

STEP 2

Decorate one side of each card. Swipe the glue stick on the undecorated sides of two cards. Take your first scented item and sprinkle or place it on the glue.

Repeat **step 2** to attach each scent to two cards.

STEP 3

To play the game, mix up the cards and arrange them scent side down on a table. Close your eyes. Then flip two cards and sniff them. If the cards are a match, leave them face up. If not, put them back. Continue until you've matched all six scents!

WHAT YOU GET

Nose neurons. Your nose is home to millions of sensory neurons. Each neuron has a protein called an olfactory receptor. The receptors detect odor molecules. Neurons then send information about the odors to your brain. This allows you to experience the smell! **That's science!**

DIY TEA SOAP

Turn tea leaves into a soap that cleans and smells **beau-tea-ful!**

WHAT YOU NEED

- bar of soap
- cheese grater

- bowl
- tea bag
- cup of hot water
- scissors
- fork
- spoon
- silicon ice cube trays

PRICKLY PEAR CACTUS

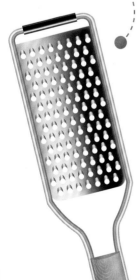

STEP 1

Use the cheese grater to grate the soap into a bowl.

STEP 2

Set the tea bag in a cup of hot water for several minutes.

STEP 3

Pour the water into the bowl of soap. Cut open the tea bag and dump the leaves into the bowl. Let the bowl sit for about 30 minutes so the water soaks into the soap flakes.

30 MIN

STEP 4

Mash the mixture together with a fork. Spoon it into ice cube trays and press down with the back of the spoon. Let the trays sit overnight.

STEP 5

Pop the soaps out of the trays. Use one to wash your hands!

WHAT YOU GET

Amazing molecules. Soap molecules have two ends. The head is attracted to water. The tail is attracted to oils and fats. In dirty water, soap molecules form clusters called micelles. The heads point outward. The tails point inward, trapping dirt and grease inside the micelle. The micelles wash away when rinsed with water. **That's science!**

BIRTHDAY BATTER SLIME

SMELL-O-METER 4

Mix up a **sweet-smelling slime** worthy of a celebration!

WHAT YOU NEED

- hole punch
- cardstock in various colors
- medium mixing bowl & spoon
- ½ cup (118 mL) school glue
- ½ cup (118 mL) water
- ½ teaspoon (2.5 mL) vanilla extract
- ¾ cup (177 mL) liquid starch

Pure Vanilla Extract

▲ ▲ ▲

EXPERIMENT! WHAT OTHER SCENTS COULD YOU ADD TO SLIME? HOW DO THEY AFFECT THE SLIME'S LOOK AND FEEL?

▼ ▼ ▼

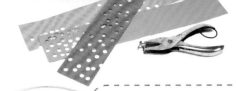

STEP 1

Use the hole punch to cut confetti out of the cardstock.

STEP 2

In a medium mixing bowl, mix together the glue and water.

STEP 3

Add the vanilla and confetti. Mix well.

STEP 4

Add ½ cup (118 mL) liquid starch. Knead the mixture until the slime is smooth and no longer sticks to your hands. If your slime stays sticky, add up to ¼ cup (59 mL) more starch. Close your eyes and smell the slime!

WHAT YOU GET

Slimy, smelly molecules.
Glue is made of long chains of molecules. The molecules flow past each other. Liquid starch causes the glue molecules to link together. This makes the glue thick and rubbery! Adding vanilla infuses the slime with odor molecules. **That's science!**

SCENT SCRAPBOOK

Discover the powerful connection between scent and memory by creating an **odor-iffic** scrapbook!

SMELL-O-METER
6

Scrapbook

Great memories in smell

WHAT YOU NEED

- scented objects, such as pine needles, fresh cut grass, or scented lotion
- paper
- scissors
- hole punch
- art supplies, such as markers, crayons, colored pencils & glue
- brass brad

STEP 1

Collect scented items that remind you of specific memories, places, or events. Items could include pine needles, fresh cut grass, or scented lotion.

STEP 2

Cut several sheets of paper in half. Stack the papers. Punch a hole in the top left corner of the stack. This is your scrapbook. Make a cover.

STEP 3

On each inside page, draw a picture of the memory represented by each scent. Use glue to add the scented item into the image.

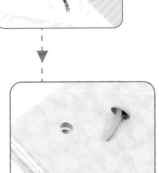

STEP 4

Push a brad through the hole to secure the pages together. Look through the scrapbook without smelling. Repeat, but this time inhale deeply as you look at each page. What do you notice?

WHAT YOU GET

Brain power. Scent has a stronger link to memory than any other sense. Scents are processed in your brain's olfactory bulb. This is directly connected to the parts of your brain that process emotions and memory. **That's science!**

CALMING CRAYON CANDLE

SMELL-O-METER

Turn old art supplies into a relaxing candle that gives off a **calming scent** as it burns.

EXPERIMENT! TRY ADDING DIFFERENT TYPES OF ESSENTIAL OILS TO DIFFERENT LAYERS.

WHAT YOU NEED

- candle wick
- scissors
- 50–100 old crayons
- craft knife
- glass bowl that can sit on top of a saucepan
- aluminum foil
- saucepan
- water
- whisk
- essential oil in a calming scent
- glass jar
- lighter, matches, or candle warmer

STEP 1

Cut the wick a few inches longer than the jar is deep. Use a craft knife to slice vertically down a crayon wrapper. Peel the wrapper off. Repeat for each crayon.

STEP 2

Line a glass bowl with aluminum foil. Break similarly colored crayons into pieces and place in the bowl.

STEP 3

Pour a few inches of water into a saucepan and bring to a simmer. Set the glass bowl on top of the pan. Allow the crayons to melt.

STEP 4

Remove the pan from heat. Whisk a few drops of essential oil into the bowl.

STEP 5

Pour the melted wax into the jar. Put one end of the wick into the jar. Hold the top while the wax cools.

Repeat **steps 2 through 5** to add additional layers.

STEP 6

Light your candle. What happens?

WHAT YOU GET

Smell release. As the candle burns, the wax melts. The essential oil in the heated wax turns into gas. When a substance turns into gas, it releases more odor molecules. So, the burning candle has a strong smell. **That's science!**

SEASON IN A JAR

What does spring smell like to you? Capture the scents of each season in a jar you can sniff anytime!

WHAT YOU NEED

- scented items, such as cinnamon sticks, flower petals & leaves
- 4 jars with lids
- art supplies (optional)

▲ ▲ ▲

EXPERIMENT! ASK ANOTHER PERSON TO CLOSE THEIR EYES AND SMELL YOUR SEASON JARS. CAN THEY GUESS THE SEASON?

▼ ▼ ▼

STEP 1

Collect items that remind you of each season, such as orange peels for winter or flower petals for spring.

STEP 2

Place each season's items in a separate jar.

STEP 3

Put the lids on the jars. Decorate each jar if you'd like.

STEP 4

Close your eyes. Open each jar one at a time and breathe in the scent. What do you experience?

WHAT YOU GET

So many scents! A human nose has more than 400 types of olfactory receptors. These allow us to detect more than 1 trillion different scents. Many seasonal scents bring up memories of holidays and other experiences. **That's science!**

NOT-SO-STINKY SOCK

Aromatherapy means using natural, strongly scented oils to improve well-being. Explore **aromatherapy** as you turn an old sock into a sweet-smelling pal.

WHAT YOU NEED

- 3–4 cups (0.7–1 L) rice
- bowl
- essential oil
- spoon
- funnel
- sock
- twine
- art supplies that can safely be microwaved, such as felt & fabric glue
- microwave

EXPERIMENT! TRY THIS PROJECT USING OTHER SCENTS. DO YOU NOTICE A DIFFERENCE IN HOW YOU FEEL?

STEP 1

Pour the rice into a bowl. Add a few drops of essential oil and stir until the rice is coated.

STEP 2

Use a funnel to pour the rice into the sock.

STEP 3

Shake the sock so the rice settles to the bottom. Pinch the sock a few inches above the rice. Tie with a piece of twine to secure. Decorate your sock!

STEP 4

Microwave your sock buddy in 30-second bursts until it is warm but not hot. Note how you feel. Now hold the sock close and breathe in the scent. Did your feelings change?

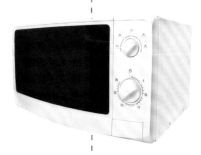

WHAT YOU GET

A mood changer. Certain odors are thought to help you feel better. When inhaled, the smells cause a certain response in the brain. Lavender helps some people feel calm. A lemon scent may be able to improve your mood. **That's science!**

SCRATCH & SNIFF PAINT

Mix up some scented paints to create a picture that **smells as good** as it looks!

WHAT YOU NEED

- white school glue
- paint palette or egg carton
- food coloring
- craft sticks
- liquid scents, such as essential oils, almond extract & lemon juice
- paintbrush & paper

STEP 1

Squeeze the glue into each palette cup. If you don't have a palette, use an egg carton.

STEP 2

Add a few drops of food coloring to each palette cup. Use craft sticks to stir in the food coloring.

STEP 3

Add a few drops of scent to each color. Use different scents for each one. Stir in the scents with craft sticks.

STEP 4

Paint a picture and let it dry. Scratch each color with your fingernail. What happens?

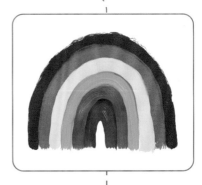

WHAT YOU GET

A scent masterpiece! When you scratch the dried paint, the paint releases odor molecules into the air. The molecules are detected by the neurons in your nose. They send information about the scent to your brain. **That's science!**

STINKY SNEAKER SWAB

SMELL-O-METER 8

Does stinky really mean dirty? Find out by using your **stinkiest sneakers** to grow a bacteria garden.

WHAT YOU NEED

- old, stinky sneakers
- clean sneakers
- 2 cotton swabs
- 2 petri dishes with agar
- tape
- marker

EXPERIMENT! REPEAT THIS PROJECT WITH OTHER STINKY ITEMS, SUCH AS THE INSIDE OF A GARBAGE CAN.

STEP 1

Swab the inside of a stinky sneaker with a clean cotton swab.

STEP 2

Lightly rub the swab back and forth in a zig-zag motion along the agar in a petri dish.

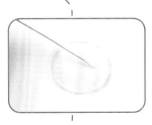

Repeat **steps 1 and 2** with the clean sneakers.

STEP 3

Use tape and a marker to label each petri dish with the type of sneaker. Allow the petri dishes to sit in a warm place.

STEP 4

Check on your petri dishes each day for 2 weeks. What do you notice? Which petri dish grows more bacteria?

2 WEEKS

NEW   OLD

WHAT YOU GET

Bacteria at work. A human foot contains 125,000 sweat glands. The mix of sweat and the warm, damp environment of the shoe makes a perfect place for bacteria to grow. When the bacteria break down the sweat, they release a strong and stinky odor. **That's science!**

FLOWER POWER

Find out which flowers attract which pollinators and **what scent has to do with it!**

SMELL-O-METER

WHAT YOU NEED

- 2 flowers of the same color, 1 with a strong scent and 1 with little to no scent
- 2 vases or jars of water
- notebook
- pencil

EXPERIMENT! TRY PUTTING DIFFERENT SCENTS, SUCH AS VANILLA OR LEMON, ON COTTON BALLS AND LEAVING THEM OUTSIDE. WHAT HAPPENS?

STEP 1

Collect two flowers of the same color, one scented and one unscented, such as a white daisy and a gardenia.

STEP 2

Place each flower in a vase or jar of water.

STEP 3

Set the flowers outside in a warm, sunny green space. The flowers should be about 10 feet (3 meters) apart from each other.

STEP 4

Observe your flowers every 10 to 15 minutes for several hours. Take notes on which pollinators, such as bees, wasps, and butterflies, visit which flowers. Does one flower get more visitors than the other?

WHAT YOU GET

Pollinator preference. Most plants use their scent to attract pollinators. Flies and bees prefer sweet scents. Beetles prefer musty, fruity, or spicy scents. A plant's scent is strongest when it is ready for pollination. **That's science!**

SLITHERING SLIME

Magnets can make objects move. Use the force of magnetism to cause slime to **creep across a table!**

WHAT YOU NEED

- ⅓ cup (79 mL) school glue
- 3 tablespoons (44 mL) iron oxide powder
- mixing bowl & spoon
- ¼ cup (59 mL) liquid starch
- rubber or latex gloves
- neodymium magnets

STEP 1

Mix the school glue and iron oxide powder together in a bowl.

STEP 2

Add the liquid starch to the school glue and iron oxide mixture. Stir until the mixture begins to thicken.

STEP 3

Put on gloves. Mix the slime with your hands until it is no longer sticky.

STEP 4

Put the slime on your work surface. Set a magnet near the slime. Watch the slime move!

WHAT YOU GET

Magnetism! Magnetism is a force that makes certain metals move toward each other. Iron is a metal. So is the neodymium magnet. Magnets are surrounded by a magnetic field. When slime enters the field, the iron oxide is pulled toward the magnet. **That's science!**

SUPER SAILBOAT

Build a plastic bottle boat and use electricity to send it zipping **across the water!**

MOVE-O-METER

WHAT YOU NEED

- plastic water bottle
- craft knife
- battery holder & batteries
- wire stripper
- motorized micro propeller
- electrical tape
- art supplies
- tub or sink filled with water

EXPERIMENT! WHAT ELSE COULD YOU USE FOR THE HULLS? IS THERE A BETTER PLACE TO PUT THE BATTERY HOLDER?

STEP 1

Cut the neck off the bottle. Cut the bottle in half lengthwise. These are the boat's hulls.

STEP 2

Strip the coating off the ends of the battery holder's wires. Wrap the ends around the connectors on the motor.

STEP 3

Tape the motor between the hulls so the post sticks out behind the boat. Tape the battery holder inside one hull.

STEP 4

Decorate the boat if you'd like. Put the propeller on the motor. Set the boat in water. Make sure the propeller is in the water and the motor is not. Turn on the motor and watch your boat go!

WHAT YOU GET

The power of electricity! Connecting the wires from the batteries to the motor completes a circuit. The circuit lets electricity flow from the batteries to the motor and back. This electricity powers the motor and turns the propeller. **That's science!**

CANDY CATAPULT

Study forces and motion by launching objects with a mini catapult. **You can make candy fly!**

WHAT YOU NEED

- shoebox
- scissors
- ruler
- art supplies
- pushpin
- 2 pencils longer than the box's width
- 2 rubber bands
- hot glue gun
- chenille stem
- plastic bottle cap
- gumdrops or other small candies

STEP 1

Cut a large rectangular hole in the shoebox's lid. Leave about 1 inch (2.5 cm) at each end. Tape the lid in place if necessary. Decorate the shoebox.

STEP 2

Poke a pushpin into one long side of the box, about ½ inch (1.2 cm) from the top and 3 inches (8 cm) from one end.

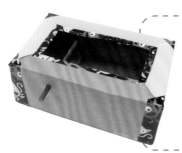

STEP 3

Push a pencil through the hole to the other side of the box. Poke a hole in that side for the pencil to go through.

STEP 4

Use a rubber band to secure the second pencil to the middle of the first in a cross shape. About 2 inches (5 cm) of the second pencil should stick down below the first pencil.

Continued on the next page.

▶▶▶

STEP 5

Cut the second rubber band. Tie one end to the second pencil below the first pencil. Hot glue can help hold the rubber band in place.

STEP 6

In the end of the box opposite the pencils, poke a hole 1 inch (2.5 cm) up from the bottom.

STEP 7

String the loose end of the cut rubber band through the hole. Pull until the rubber band is tight. Tie the end around a small piece of chenille stem.

STEP 8

Hot glue a plastic bottle cap to the top of the second pencil. The inside of the cap should face away from the stretched rubber band.

STEP 9

Pull the end of the pencil with the cap down toward the box. Set a piece of candy in the cap. Let go and watch the candy fly!

▲ ▲ ▲
EXPERIMENT! TRY USING DIFFERENT TYPES OF CANDY AND OTHER OBJECTS. WHICH FLIES THE FARTHEST?
▼ ▼ ▼

WHAT YOU GET

Energy transfer! Every object has potential energy. This means it could move in the right conditions. Moving objects have kinetic energy. When you pull the pencil down, the rubber band has potential energy. When you let go, kinetic energy from the rubber band transfers to the object, shooting it through the air. The object has kinetic energy while it is flying. **That's science!**

RUBBER BAND TRUCK

This monster truck doesn't need fuel to go. It's powered by a rubber band!

WHAT YOU NEED

- cardboard box
- art supplies
- 2 wooden skewers
- ruler
- pencil
- drinking straws
- scissors
- hot glue gun
- rubber band
- paper clip
- 4 empty tape tubes
- cardboard
- duct tape
- pushpin
- small box (optional)

STEP 1

Decorate the cardboard box. This will be the body of your truck. Make sure you can still access the inside of the box.

STEP 2

Use a wooden skewer to poke two holes through one long side of the box. The holes should be about 1 inch (2.5 cm) from each end. Poke two holes through the box's other side. Make sure the holes line up with those on the first side.

STEP 3

Use a pencil to make the holes big enough for the straws to fit through. Cut four straw pieces that are each about 2 inches (5 cm) long. Push a straw piece through each hole. Use hot glue to hold them in place.

STEP 4

Slide a wooden skewer through each pair of straws. These are the truck's axles.

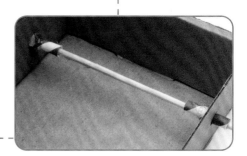

Continued on the next page.

STEP 5

Loop a rubber band around one skewer. Loop the other end of the rubber band around a paper clip. Attach the paper clip to the closest short end of the box. Close the box lid and secure it shut.

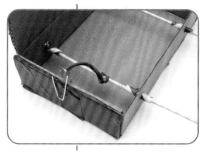

STEP 6

Trace the inside of a tape tube four times on cardboard. Cut out the circles. Decorate them if you like.

STEP 7

Wrap each tape tube in duct tape. Fit a cardboard circle inside each tube. Trim the circles if necessary and glue them in place. These are the truck's wheels.

STEP 8

Use a pushpin to poke a hole in the center of each wheel. Use a pencil to make the holes big enough for the skewers to fit through. Push each wheel onto the end of a skewer.

STEP 9

If you'd like, decorate a second, smaller box. Add it to the top of your truck to make the cab.

STEP 10

Set the truck on an even surface. Roll it backward until the wheels won't turn anymore. Let go of the truck. Watch it zoom away!

WHAT YOU GET

Elastic action! Rubber bands are elastic. This means they stretch when pulled. Stretched rubber bands store potential energy. Pulling the truck back causes the rubber band to wrap around the axle and stretch. When you let the truck go, the rubber band snaps back in place, converting the potential energy into kinetic energy. This energy makes the truck go! **That's science!**

ZOOM BOTTLE BLASTOFF

MOVE-O-METER 6

Harness the power of inertia to make your own zoom bottle.
How fast can you make it zip?

WHAT YOU NEED

- 2 water bottles
- scissors
- tape
- string
- ruler
- art supplies
- partner

▲ ▲ ▲

**EXPERIMENT!
WHAT HAPPENS IF YOU CHANGE THE LENGTH OF THE STRINGS? OR IF ONE PERSON RAISES THEIR END HIGHER?**

▼ ▼ ▼

STEP 1

Cut the top half off each bottle.
Tape them together at the center.

STEP 2

Cut two pieces of string 10 to
12 feet (3 to 4 meters) long. Tie
a large loop in each end of both
strings. Thread the strings through
the bottle. Decorate the bottle.

STEP 3

Hold the loops on one side. Hold one loop
in each hand. Have a partner hold the
loops on the other side. Back away from
each other until the strings are tight.

STEP 4

The person nearest the bottle should
snap their strings apart. The bottle will
zoom away! Have the other person bring
their strings together as the bottle comes
near. Then they can snap their strings
apart to send the bottle back. Keep
blasting the bottle back and forth!

WHAT YOU GET

Inertia in action! Objects don't move unless a force makes
them. They then keep moving until a new force stops them.
This concept is called inertia. Separating the strings creates a
force that sends the bottle shooting forward. When the other
person separates their strings, that force sends the bottle
zooming in the other direction. **That's science!**

WHIRLING FROG

Use electricity and force to create a friendly frog that **whirls, shakes, and jitters!**

WHAT YOU NEED

- AAA battery holder with switch & batteries
- wire stripper
- 1.5–3 V mini motor
- pencil with eraser
- scissors
- CD
- hot glue gun
- duct tape
- craft foam
- googly eyes
- markers

STEP 1

Strip the coating off the ends of the battery holder's wires. Wrap the ends around the connectors on the motor.

STEP 2

Cut the eraser off a pencil. Press the eraser onto the motor's post.

STEP 3

Set the motor on the CD so the eraser sticks through the hole. Hot glue the motor in place.

STEP 4

Tape the battery holder next to the motor on the CD. Cover the CD with duct tape.

STEP 5

Cut a frog out of craft foam. Use googly eyes, tape, and markers to add details.

STEP 6

Hot glue the bottom edge of the frog to the CD. Let the glue dry. Set the frog on a hard floor. Turn on the motor. Watch the frog spin!

WHAT YOU GET

Friction! Friction is a force that acts between two objects rubbing against each other. When the motor is turned on, the eraser rubs against the floor. The friction between the eraser and the floor makes the frog jump and turn. **That's science!**

BUZZING BUG BOTS

Construct a swarm of robot bugs. They'll **create a lot of buzz!**

WHAT YOU NEED

- toothbrushes with flat bristles
- tin snips
- mini vibrating motors with wires
- wire stripper
- hot glue gun
- button batteries
- tape
- chenille stems
- scissors
- googly eyes

STEP 1

Use tin snips to cut the head off a toothbrush. Strip the coating off the ends of a motor's wires.

STEP 2

Glue the motor to the top of a battery. Glue the bottom of the battery to the toothbrush head.

STEP 3

Tape one of the wires to the bottom of the battery. Cut a short piece of chenille stem. Fold it into a V shape. Glue the chenille stem to the front of the toothbrush head. Glue googly eyes to the chenille stem.

Repeat **steps 1 through 3** to make more bug bots.

STEP 4

When your swarm is ready, set the bots on a hard, flat surface. Tape the top wires to the batteries. Watch your bots buzz!

WHAT YOU GET

Circuits and friction! The wires form a circuit that lets electricity flow between the battery and the motor. This electricity makes the bot vibrate. The vibrations create friction between the bristles and the flat surface. This friction propels the bots across the surface. **That's science!**

TWIRLING RAINBOW

Colors are on the move with this spinner! Twirl the dowel and watch the rainbow **expand and contract.**

WHAT YOU NEED

- paper in six colors
- scissors
- ruler
- hole punch
- wooden dowel
- pushpin

EXPERIMENT!
WHAT HAPPENS TO THE STRIPS OF PAPER WHEN YOU SPIN THE DOWEL FASTER? WHAT HAPPENS IF YOU USE LONGER STRIPS OF PAPER?

STEP 1

Cut two strips of each color paper. Make each strip 1¼ by 11 inches (3 by 28 cm).

STEP 2

Punch a hole near one end of each strip. Make sure the dowel fits easily through the holes.

STEP 3

Stack the strips in rainbow order. Line up the holes. Push the dowel through them. Pin the strips to the top of the dowel.

STEP 4

Fan out the strips to form a ball. Rotate the dowel and watch the colors spin!

WHAT YOU GET

Centrifugal force! This force causes a rotating object to move away from the center of its rotation. The dowel is the center of rotation. When you rotate the dowel, centrifugal force pushes the strips of paper out to form a wider, flatter ball. **That's science!**

WHIRRING WINDMILL

Build a simple and sleek windmill to harness the **power of the wind.**

WHAT YOU NEED

- 19 large craft sticks
- hot glue gun
- paper towel tube
- large nail with a flat head
- small rubber band
- ruler
- scissors
- plastic bottle cap
- paint & paintbrushes
- electric fan

STEP 1

Lay eight craft sticks side by side. Glue eight sticks side by side across them. This forms a square base for the windmill.

STEP 2

Hot glue the paper towel tube to the middle of the base. Make sure it's secure.

STEP 3

Wrap a rubber band around a nail about ⅓ inch (1 cm) from the head. Poke the nail through the tube 1 inch (2.5 cm) from the top.

STEP 4

Cut the remaining three craft sticks in half. Hot glue the stick halves around a bottle cap so they are all slightly angled in the same direction.

STEP 5

Hot glue the nail's head to the inside of the bottle cap. Paint your windmill. Set your windmill in front of a fan. Does the windmill turn?

WHAT YOU GET

Wind power! The wind from the fan blows on the windmill blades. Because the blades are angled, the force of the wind pushes them sideways. This makes the windmill turn. **That's science!**

FLOATING TRAIN

Make your own train that hovers above the tracks. What's behind the magical motion? **Magnets!**

WHAT YOU NEED

- monopolar magnetic tape
- whiteboard eraser
- scissors
- ruler
- toilet paper tube
- glue
- art supplies
- black paper
- white tissue paper
- cardboard

STEP 1

Stick two strips of magnetic tape to the back of the whiteboard eraser. There should be ½ inch (1.2 cm) between the strips.

STEP 2

Cut the toilet paper tube lengthwise. Glue the edges to the sides of the eraser to form the train's body. Decorate the train.

STEP 3

Make a smokestack for the top of the train. Roll a small piece of black paper into a tube. Glue tissue paper on top. Glue the smokestack to the train.

STEP 4

Cut three strips of cardboard that are about 2 feet (0.6 m) long and 3½ inches (9 cm) wide.

Continued on the next page.

STEP 5

Draw two straight lines on a cardboard strip 1½ inches (4 cm) from each long side.

STEP 6

Stick two strips of magnetic tape on the cardboard strip. Line the tape up outside the pencil lines so there is ½ inch (1.2 cm) between the magnets.

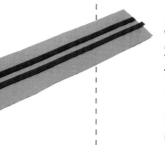

STEP 7

Fold the remaining cardboard strips lengthwise so each fold is 1 inch (2.5 cm) from one side.

STEP 8

Place the thinner flaps of the folded cardboard strips on the first strip. Line them up so the folded edges are parallel to the magnets. Glue down the thin flaps. The wider flaps should stick up straight.

STEP 9

Place the train on the track.
Push it gently and watch it float!

**EXPERIMENT!
TRY ADDING EXTRA
WEIGHT TO YOUR
TRAIN CAR. DOES IT
STILL FLOAT?**

WHAT YOU GET

Magnetic levitation! Magnets have two poles. One side is the north pole. The other side is the south pole. When matching poles of two magnets face one another, the magnets push apart. This force causes the train to hover. **That's science!**

Dabble Lab is published by Capstone Press, an imprint of Capstone.
1710 Roe Crest Drive, North Mankato, Minnesota 56003
capstonepub.com

Library of Congress Cataloging-in-Publication Data is available on the Library of Congress website.
ISBN: 9781669010982 (paperback)
ISBN: 9781669010999 (ebook PDF)

Summary: Curious kids will discover just how fun STEM can be with 49 hands-on messy, mobile, noisy, and smelly science projects.

Image Credits
iStockphoto: assalve, 5, 67 (spices), Christopher Ames, 60, 72 (essential oil and rosemary), colevineyard, 5 (soap), fcafotodigital, 5, 74 (essential oils), Joe_Potato, 5, 70 (vanilla extract), lucop, 85 (gardenia in vase); malerapaso, Front Cover, 5 (herbs), marilyna, 5, 76 (wildflowers), Photographer, 5 (crayons); Shutterstock: Africa Studio, 5, 16 (cornstarch), 84, 85 (chamomile flowers), Agave Studio, 72 (white flowers), akiyoko, 27 (acrylic paint), alarich, 5 (yarn), Aleksandr178, 5, 100 (wire stripper), Anastasia_ Panait, 48 (feathers), Andrei Dubadzel, 8 (yeast), andRiU92, 5 (batteries), Apple_Mac, 5, 10 (measuring cups & spoons), arslaan, 52 (speaker), arsslawa, 5, 54 (rubber bands), Ascannio, 20 (putty), Blan-k, 59 (music notes), Bohdan Populov, 42 (radar waves), Butterfly Hunter, 85 (butterfly), cameilia, 84 (gardenias), ChristianChan, 66 (question marks), conzorb, 64, 79 (microwave), Craig Walton, 111 (magnets), Daniel Prudek, 84, 85 (bee), Denis Dryashkin, 106 (nail), Denphumi, 80 (paintbrushes), dezign56, 66 (glue stick), diy13,11 (white bottle), Dmitriy Kazitsyn, 28 (ice pack), ehtesham, 84 (bee on flower), Ekaterina43, 56 (hook-and-loop tape), 58 (bobby pins), Elizabeth A.Cummings, 5, 8, 12, 28, 44, 80 (food coloring), Endeavor, 5, 30 (mixing bowl), focal point, 5 (baking soda), Free Life Design, 77 (orange peel), Freer, 74 (matchbox), Igartist 79, 52 (eggs), J u n e, 5, 12, 30 (mixing spoon), jultud, 23 (safety glasses), JUN3, 20 (tape), Kalfa, 63 (rotten fruit), kenary820, 10 (saline solution), koosen, 78 (rice in bowl), kubais, Front Cover (blue paint), Love the wind, 4, 17 (glitter), Lukas Gojda, 80 (painted background), Lunik MX, Back Cover, 60, 61 (bubbles), MakroBetz, 72 (brass brads), marla dawn studio, 44, 45 (metal spoon), Marxstudio, 38 (tape), Mega Pixel, 5, 14 (clear glue), 70 (school glue), 81 (rainbow picture), Mona Makela, 86 (iron oxide), Na be lazy, 42 (marbles and dice), Napat, 24 (funnel), Natakorn Ruangrit, 5, 38, 98 (scissors), New Africa, 19 (baking soda), Noel V. Baebler, 8 (hydrogen peroxide), oksana2010, 18 (chalk), Olha Solodenko, 28 (blow-dryer), ONYXprj, Front Cover, Back Cover (background), optimarc, 102 (pipe cleaners), OttoPles, 108 (tape), P-Square Studio, 40 (paper cup), paranut, 50 (paper roll), Passakorn sakulphan, 5 (straws), Paul Orr, 5, 104 (hole punch), PaulPaladin, 42, 43 (hex nuts), phil_berry, 78 (socks), Picsfive, 40 (string), pikepicture, 68 (grater), PrimaStockPhoto, 5, 98 (ruler), Purple Clouds, 86 (black slime), Regine Poirier, 66 (dryer sheets), Ricardo Javier, 86 (magnets), Rok Breznik, 5, 100 (motor), Sarah2, 69 (tea bag), Scarabea, 5, 40 (cups connected by string), Schankz, Front Cover, 18 (splotch), Sergei Bogachov, 5, 58, 62, 94 (glue gun), Sheila Fitzgerald, 80 (almond extract), showcake, 107 (fan), Simone Andress, 73 (fir needles), stuar, 5 (dish soap), sulit.photos, 16 (borax), Svitlana Martynova, 50, 106 (paintbrush), SweetLemons, 34, 62, 100 (googly eyes), Thesamphotography, 80 (lemon), thoughtsofjoyce, 60 (glycerin), timquo, 25 (filled balloons), titov dmitriy, 5 (paper cup), Valenty, 56 (sound wave), Vandathai, 17 (chalk powder), Vera NewSib, 22 (watermelon), virtu studio, 62 (eggs), Vitaly Zorkin, 54 (pencil), Vladimirkarp, 72 (pine branch), VRVIRUS, 18, 19 (hammer), wk1003mike, 5, 24, 54 (balloons), Worraratch Chinboon, 5, 15, 31 (liquid starch), Yellow Cat, 26 (blue toy dinosaur), Zerbor, 36 (bells)

Design Elements
Shutterstock: MicroOne (gauges), WhiteBarbie (calendar date)

All project photos shot by Mighty Media, Inc.

Editorial Credits
Editor: Jessica Rusick
Designer: Aruna Rangarajan